Hello. My name is Mr Gr[e]

The English language and
for quite some time now. E
at a place called 'school',   ...people tried to
teach me to read phonetically, but I was fascinated by multiple
meanings and wordplay.

Back to the not so distant past, I was looking for a theme for
an exhibition. I had written down three words: 'Butterfly',
'Ladybird' and 'Cricket'. In the first two words I could see two
words; butter + fly and lady + bird, so I looked at cricket and
thought well it has two meanings - it's an insect and a sport -
but maybe there are other words that can be broken in two and
still read as complete words in their own right.

I started to hear these words in conversations and I would note
them down. In no time I had hundreds, including a full A to Z.
I swapped the idea of an exhibition for pages and compiled the
book that's in your hands.

This book is here to help you think beyond the basics; A is for
Apple, B is for Balloon, and to understand that not everything
is as it first seems.

A IS FOR APPLE

B IS FOR BALLOON

C IS FOR CAR

D IS FOR DOG

E IS FOR EGG

F IS FOR FISH

G IS FOR GUITAR

H IS FOR HOUSE

I IS FOR IGLOO

J IS FOR JELLY

K IS FOR KEY

L IS FOR LEMON

M IS FOR MOUTH

N IS FOR NAIL

O IS FOR ORANGE

P IS FOR PENCIL

Q IS FOR QUEEN

R IS FOR RABBIT

S IS FOR STAR

T IS FOR TRAIN

U IS FOR UMBRELLA

V IS FOR VEST

W IS FOR WATER

X IS FOR XYLOPHONE

Y IS FOR YACHT

Z IS FOR ZEBRA

SO YOU'VE LEARNED YOUR A TO Z OF WORDS?

TWORDS

A TWORD IS A WORD THAT CONTAINS TWO OTHERS.

THESE TWO WORDS HAVE DIFFERENT MEANINGS FROM THE ORIGINAL TWORD.

LET ME EXPLAIN. TAKE THE WORD BREAKFAST.

TWORD: BREAKFAST
IS THE FIRST AND MOST IMPORTANT MEAL OF THE DAY.

WORD 1: BREAK
IS TO SMASH OR SPLIT SOMETHING INTO BITS.

WORD 2: FAST
IS TO GET GOING QUICKLY.

GOT IT? EASY, ISN'T IT? LETS GET STARTED!

Armband *is an inflatable band that you wear around each arm to help you float. That's because swimming is great - a bit like flying in water - but sinking isn't fun.*

A IS FOR ARM-BAND

Arm *is the bit between your shoulder and your wrist. Take a look down to your left or right. There it is!*

Band *is a type of gang that plays musical instruments. Sometimes they sing and dance too.*

A is the 1st letter in the alphabet.

Butterfly *is a fluttery, flapping, flying insect with a thin body and colourful patterned wings.*

B IS FOR BUTTER- FLY

B is the 2nd letter in the alphabet.

Butter *is the fatty yellow stuff that's made from milk and tastes good on bread and toast.*

Fly *is a small two-winged insect that likes to land on food, bins and poo.*

Cowboy *is a man who looks after cattle on a ranch. You'll find him in the Wild West and at the cinema, often riding a horse.*

C IS FOR COW-BOY

C is the 3rd letter in the alphabet.

Cow is the name for adult female cattle. They make milk, say 'moo' and sometimes sleep standing up.

"moo" moooh!"

Boy is a male human being who isn't yet fully grown. You might be one of these.

Donkey *is a domesticated member of the horse family. You can ride them at the seaside, if you ask nicely.*

D IS FOR DON-KEY

Don *is a teacher at a college or university. This means that they're very clever and brilliant at playing Trivial Pursuit.*

THE STAFF ROOM

Key *is a small piece of metal specially cut to open or close a lock. Don't lose it!*

D is the 4th letter in the alphabet.

Earwig *is a creepy crawly with large pincers on its bum.*
You can often find them hanging out under rocks.

E IS FOR EAR - WIG

E is the 5th letter in the alphabet.

Ear *is the flappy thing on the side of your head that picks up sounds and sends noises to your brain.*

Wig *is artificial hair you can wear, sometimes as a disguise, sometimes as fancy dress, and sometimes to cover a bald head.*

Foxglove *is a flower with colourful petals on a tall green stalk.*

F IS FOR FOX-GLOVE

Fox *is a member of the dog family. They have red hair and big bushy tails.*

Glove *is a covering for the hand that keeps them warm in the winter or dry when you do the dishes. You have done the dishes, haven't you?*

F is the 6th letter in the alphabet.

G IS FOR GOOSE - BERRY

Gooseberry is a hairy little fruit that grows on bushes. They're delicious in a pie for dessert, but only if you've eaten your dinner first.

Goose *is a bird that swims. It has a long neck and webbed feet, a bit like a duck.*

Berry *is a small juicy fruit, like strawberries, blueberries and blackberries. They taste good as a smoothie, with ice cream, even on their own.*

G is the 7th letter in the alphabet.

Honeycomb *is made up of row upon row of little hexagons that bees build to store their honey.*

H IS FOR HONEY-COMB

Honey *is a sweet sticky liquid. Clever bees make it using nectar from flowers.*

Honey

A TWORD PRODUCT

Comb *is a strip of plastic, wood or metal with thin teeth, used for rearranging your hair. We all like to look our best, after all.*

⬤ **H is the 8th letter in the alphabet.**

Important *is something that's really significant that you wouldn't want to miss, like your birthday.*

TOP SECRET

IMPORTANT

IMPORTANT

I IS FOR IMPORT-ANT

Import *is something that's brought into this country from another one, usually to sell.*

IMPORT

IMPORT

Ant *is a very small insect that's often black, but also red, brown or yellow. Each one has an important job to do and they love to work hard. Not good in your pants.*

I is the 9th letter in the alphabet.

Jellyfish *is a wobbly sea creature with a body like an umbrella and long tentacles. Just don't try and open one if it rains.*

J IS FOR JELLY-FISH

J is the 10th letter in the alphabet.

Jelly *is a colourful, fruity, wobbly dessert that's often popular at parties.*

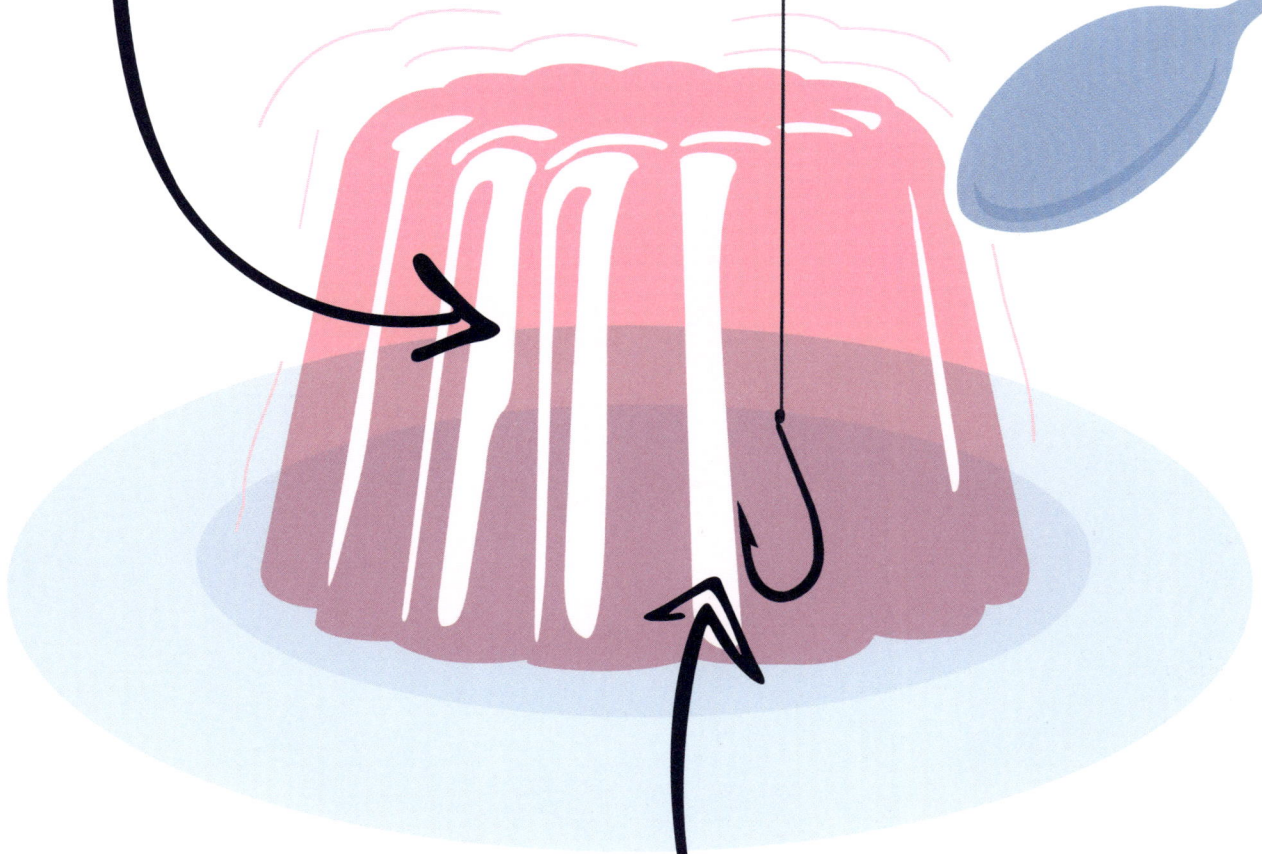

Fish *is to try to catch your dinner from the sea, a lake or maybe a pond. If you're lucky you might catch a tasty cod, if not, you might just get an old boot.*

Kingfisher *is a brilliantly coloured bird with greenish blue and yellow feathers, and like the name suggests, it's great at catching fish.*

K
IS FOR KING - FISHER

King *is the male ruler of a country. You can't apply for the job; you have to be born into the royal family first. Sorry.*

Fisher *is a man or woman that catches fish, or tries to at least.*

K is the 11th letter in the alphabet.

L IS FOR LADYBIRD

Ladybird *is a small beetle with a round spotted back.*

"Who's a pretty girl then?"

Lady *is a woman who is very polite, refined and well-mannered.*

Bird *is a warm blooded animal with feathers, wings and a beak. Most can fly, a few can swim and some even talk.*

L is the 12th letter in the alphabet.

Minimum *is the least amount possible. No more, no less.*

500 ml
400
300
200
100

M IS FOR MINI- MUM

Mini *is a small, reduced, or miniature size of anything.*

Mum *is a female parent. You should almost always do what your mum tells you.*

M is the 13th letter in the alphabet.

N IS FOR NECK-LACE

Necklace *is a piece of jewellery that you can wear around your neck. They are often made from metals like gold, and decorated with beads, jewels and pearls.*

Neck *is the part of an animal or human body that holds up your head and connects it to your body.*

Lace *is a type of string found on shoes and clothing that pulls two bits together and holds them tight.*

N is the 14th letter in the alphabet.

O
IS FOR
OFF - ICE

Office *is a place where many adults go to work.*

Off *is to move away from a place, person or thing. For example, shall we get off to the next tword?*

Ice *is a solid form of frozen water that you can skate on or put in your lemonade. Very cold!*

O is the 15th letter in the alphabet.

Pineapple *is a juicy tropical fruit with a hard spiky skin and a crown of leaves on top.*

P

IS FOR PINE - APPLE

P is the 16th letter in the alphabet.

Pine *is the wood from a pine tree.*

Apple *is a roundish red or green fruit that grows on trees. It's part of the rose family, but it's not very romantic. It is very tasty though.*

Quicksand *is a loose sand filled with water. If you stand on it you'll be sucked down below!*

DANGER

Q IS FOR QUICK-SAND

Q is the 17th letter in the alphabet.

1 HOUR

Quick *is to be fast. Don't blink or you might miss it.*

Sand *is the small grains of rock that you can feel between your toes at the beach.*

1 HOUR

Rainbow *is an arc of seven colours that appears in the sky when it's sunny and raining at the same time.*

RED
ORANGE
YELLOW
GREEN
BLUE
INDIGO
VIOLET

R IS FOR RAIN-BOW

R is the 18th letter in the alphabet.

Rain *is water that falls from the sky, often while you're out trying to have a picnic.*

Bow *is a knot with two loops and two loose ends used to tie shoes and presents.*

S IS FOR SEA-SON

Season is a period in nature that divides the year up. There are four seasons: Spring, Summer, Autumn and Winter.

Son *is a male child to his Mum and Dad.*

Sea *is the salty water that covers most of the earth's surface.*

S is the 19th letter in the alphabet.

T IS FOR TOAD-STOOL

Toadstool *is a red and white spotted mushroom that's popular with gnomes and fairies.*

T is the 20th letter in the alphabet.

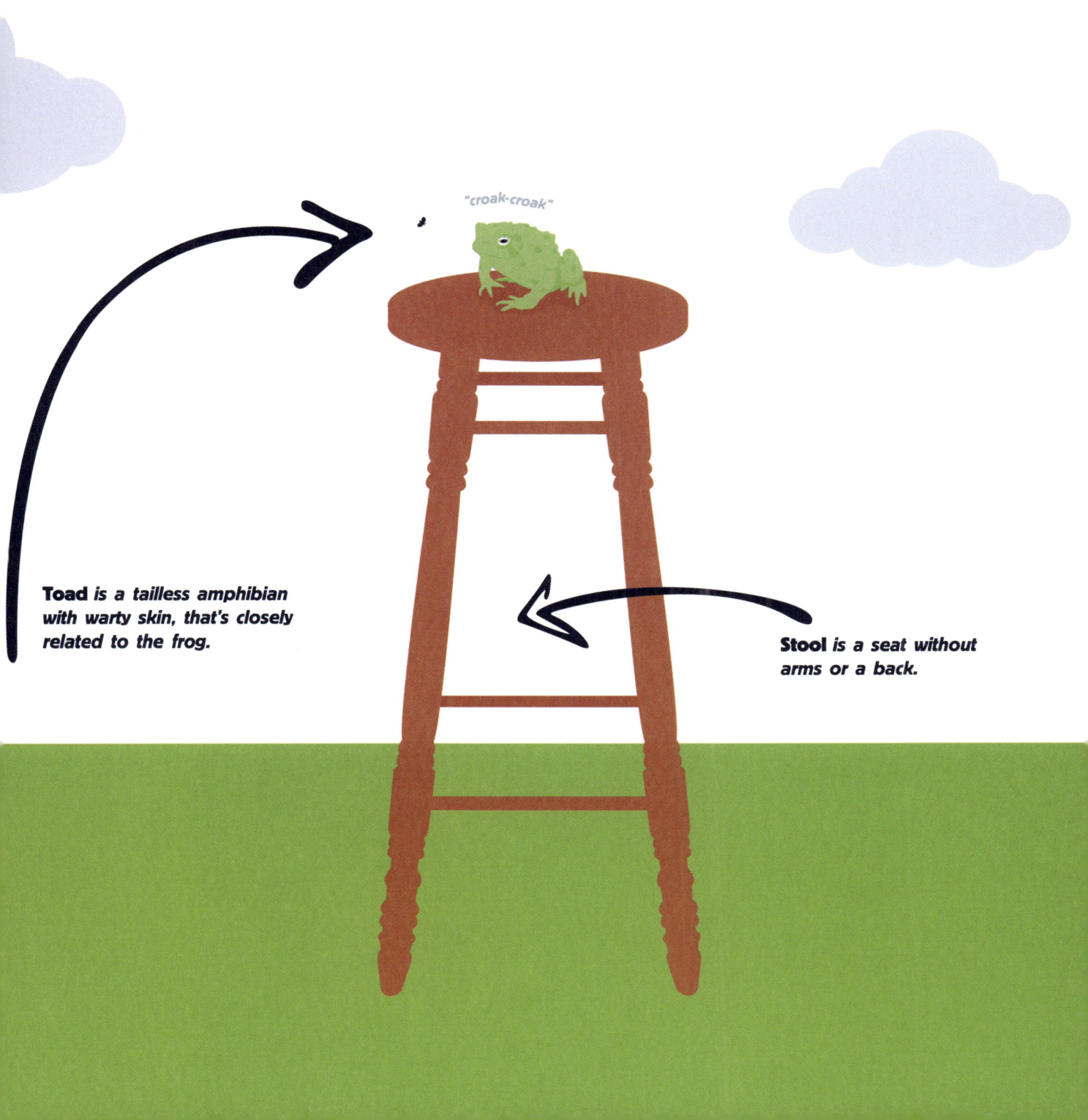

"croak-croak"

Toad *is a tailless amphibian with warty skin, that's closely related to the frog.*

Stool *is a seat without arms or a back.*

U IS FOR UNDERPANTS

Underpants *is clothing you wear under your trousers and over your bum.*

Under *is when you're below something, like a table when you're playing hide and seek.*

Pants *is what Americans call trousers.*

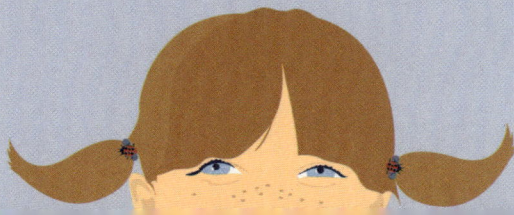

U is the 21st letter in the alphabet.

Volleyball *is a game where two teams try and keep a ball in the air while hitting it with their hands over a net.*

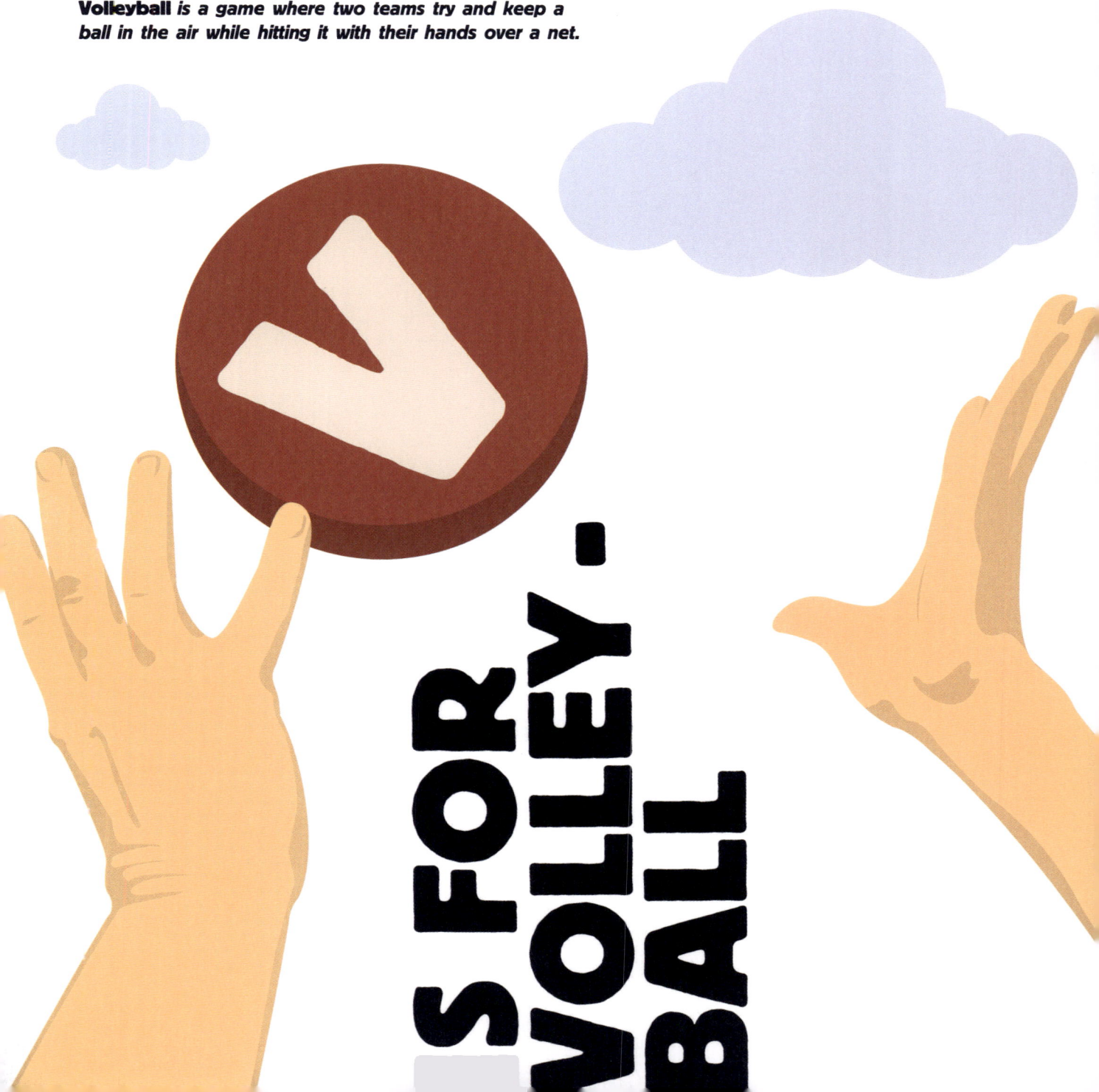

IS FOR VOLLEY-BALL

Volley *is to hit or kick something before it touches the ground.*

Ball *is a large party where people dress smartly and dance.*

V is the 22nd letter in the alphabet.

Waterfall *is a steep wall of flowing water.*

W IS FOR WATERFALL

W is the 23rd letter in the alphabet.

Water *is a transparent liquid, also known as H_2O. You can swim in it, drink it, even freeze it. Around 60% of your body is made of water.*

Fall *is to drop to the ground under the force of gravity. Which can hurt.*

X IS FOR X-RAY

X-ray is a way of photographing what's inside something or someone – even you!

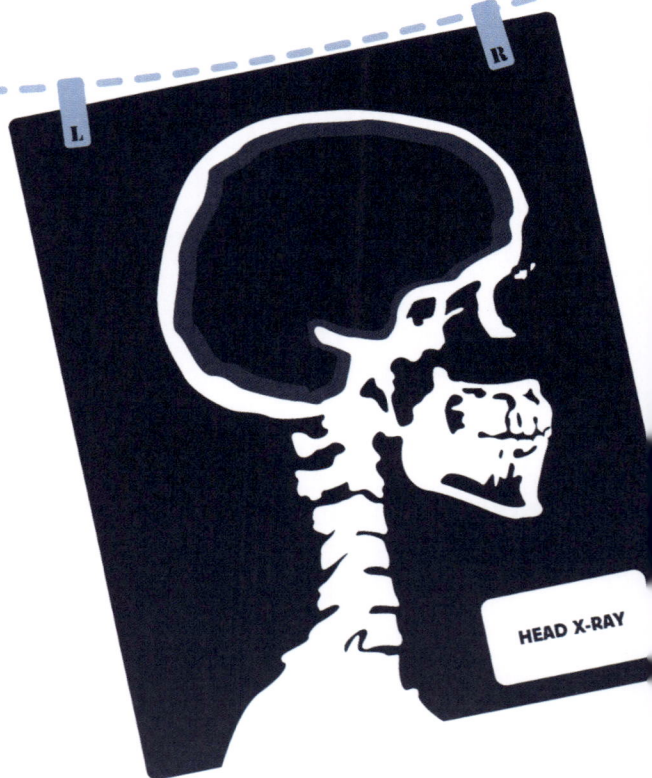

HEAD X-RAY

X is a cross shape used by pirates to mark where their treasure is buried.

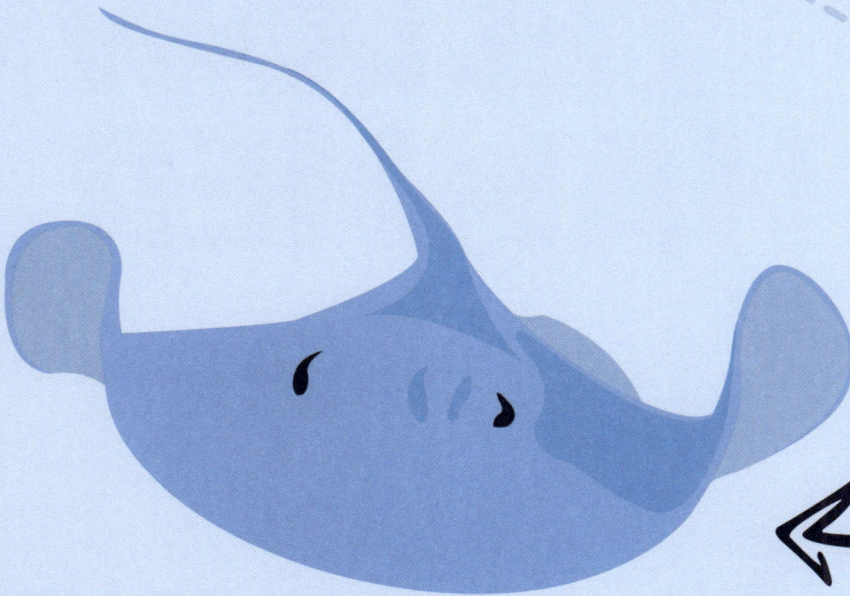

Ray is a type of fish related to sharks that lives in the ocean. Be careful of the tail — it's venomous!

X is the 24th letter in the alphabet.

Y
IS FOR YELLOW - HAMMER

Yellowhammer is a well-travelled little bird with bright yellow wings and tail.

Y is the 25th letter in the alphabet.

Yellow *is the colour between green and orange in the rainbow. It's also the colour of bananas, egg yolks and New York taxis.*

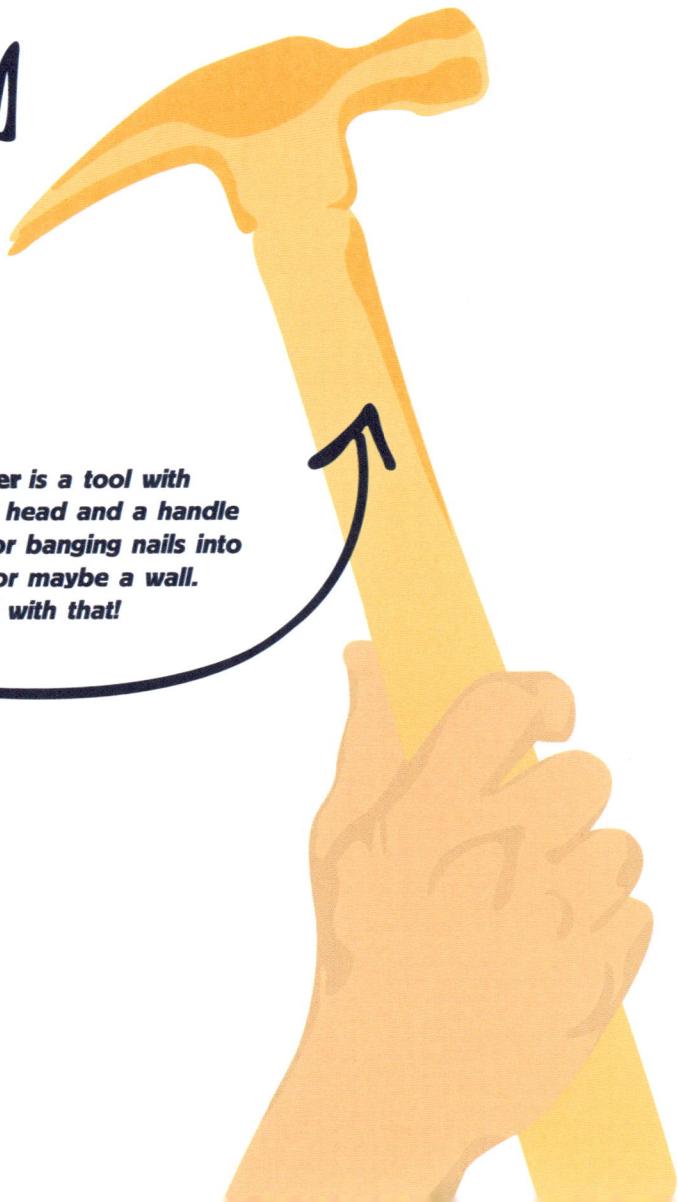

Hammer *is a tool with a solid head and a handle used for banging nails into wood or maybe a wall. Careful with that!*

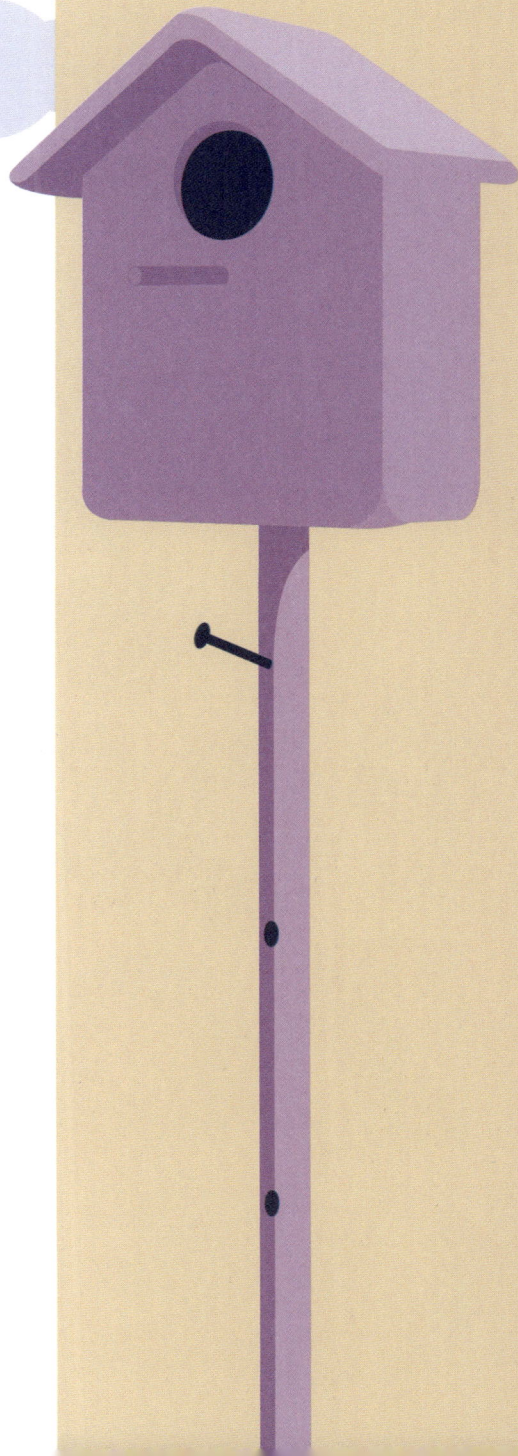

Zookeeper *is a person who looks after the animals in a zoo.*

Z

Z IS FOR ZOO- KEEPE

Zoo *is the place you go to visit collections of animals like lions, tigers and monkeys.*

ZOO

R

Keeper *is the person in a sports team who has the special job of stopping the ball cross the goal line.*

Z is the 26th letter in the alphabet.

TWORDS ARE EVERYWHERE!

AIRBUS   AIRPORT   ARMPIT   BLUEBOTTLE   BREAKFAST
CARPET   CATWALK   CHECKPOINT   CHESTNUT   CUPBOARD
DRAGONFLY   FANFARE   FIREFLY   FLIPFLOP   FREELANCE
GINGERNUT   GRASSHOPPER   GREENFLY   HAMMERHEAD
HEADBAND   HEADLINE   HEADPHONES   HEADQUARTERS
HIPHOP   HUMMINGBIRD   INSIDE   JUSTICE   KICKOFF
KINGPIN   LEAPFROG   LIFELINE   MAGPIE   MUDSKIPPER
NEEDLEWORK   OUTCAST   OUTSKIRTS   OVERRUN   PALACE
PEACOCK   QUARTERBACK   RIVERBED   ROADRUNNER
RUCKSACK   RUNWAY   SEESAW   SNAPSHOT   STARFISH
SUITCASE   TIPTOE   UNDERSTOOD   UNICORN   UPRIGHT
UPROOT   VIEWFINDER   VIEWPOINT   WEBSITE   WHIPPET
WHOLESOME   WOODPECKER   X-RATED   YARDSTICK
YEARBOOK   YOURSELF   ZIPLINE...

THE END. OR IS IT THE BEGINNING? SEE HOW MANY YOU CAN FIND TODAY.